Scarbo

on old pictu
Volu

CW01024396

Norman Ellis

3. With everyone in best Edwardian attire, this is the 'Church Parade' that customarily occurred after Sunday morning worship at church or chapel. The view from South Bay Esplanade is backed by fine hotels, including The Grand. Arthur M Cromack, photographer, 28 King Street, Scarborough, published the card.

Designed and published by Reflections of a Bygone Age, Keyworth, Nottingham 2007

Printed by Phase, Underwood, Nottingham

£3.95

4. Bathing tents feature on this panorama of South Sands. Pa and Ma posted the card from Scarborough to Blackpool. *"Glad to hear you are having a good time, so are we. A grand place, mother is walking me to death".* The card, by the Regent Publishing, London, was sent on 21 July 1925.

Front cover: *Scarborough's bright and breezy character is captured on this panorama of South Bay, showing the Grand Hotel and Old Pier with its lighthouse. Artist Hayward Young (pseudonym Jotter) provides extra effect with seagulls, sou'westers and shower clouds. Misch & Stock published the postcard in their 'Nature's Miniatures' (Scenes in Yorkshire) series.*

Back cover (top left): *The approach to historic Scarborough Castle passes the grave (second from left) of Anne Bronte, author of "The Tenant of Wildfell Hall", who died at Scarborough in 1849. The grave is in a detached part of the graveyard of St Mary's Church. The painting by JW Williams was published as a postcard by Thomas Taylor & Son of Scarborough in their 'Queen' series.*

(top right): *The Pageant of Scarborough was held in the grounds of the Castle from 9-13 July 1912. The event spawned a number of postcards, including this commemorative advert type, appropriately published by ETW Dennis & Sons, the town's own printers and postcard publishers. The back of the card carries an imprint for the Royal Hotel, situated on St Nicholas Cliff.*

(bottom): *A huge crowd watches a pierrot show on the South Sands. Note the bathing machines in the sea, and the fact that everyone is fully clothed! In the background are The Grand Hotel and Scarborough Castle. This postcard was published by the London firm Hartmann and posted to Nottingham in August 1904 with the message "thought you would like another view of Scarborough for your collection".*

Introduction

Much of the Scarborough which we see today was established by the end of the 19th century. Scarborough's medicinal waters were discovered about 1620; sea bathing was becoming popular by 1730. When the railway arrived in 1845, hotels and guest houses were already being built. The Grand Hotel dates from 1867. The pleasure pier on North Bay was completed in 1869, but the final section of the Marine Drive was not finished until 1908. The crumbling cliffs of the North and South Bays were converted into gardens and walks, and Peasholm Park was opened in 1912. Scarborough actually goes back much earlier: the medieval town was built to the south of the castle, and the adjacent harbour became a centre of activity. Here, stone piers were constructed in the 18th and early part of the 19th centuries. Shipbuilding and whaling were overshadowed by commercial fishing. 'The Queen of Watering Places' and 'The Northern Naples' were expressions used to describe the resort, in spite of the fickle weather.

Scarborough is essentially an outdoor resort, but has long managed to provide a variety of indoor attractions. It is not the only gem along Yorkshire's coastline, but for size and splendour is perhaps only matched by Whitby. The pair are, however, vastly different. The two parts of Whitby are separated by the River Esk, whereas Scarborough's two huge bays are divided by a massive headland which juts out to sea. The popularity of Scarborough led to a plethora of postcards from 1894, with the town's very own firm of ETW Dennis leading the way, publishing Britain's first commercial picture postcards in September of that year, after the Post Office gave permission for private firms to produce cards that could be posted with an adhesive stamp. From 1902, excellent work came from several local photographers.

In Edwardian days, four or five guineas would have procured a week's holiday with full board for one person at The Grand Hotel or Prince of Wales Hotel. That was a lot of money. At the other end of the scale was 'apartment' accommodation at around £1 per week, popular with working-class people up to the 1939-45 war. 'Apartments' meant you got a bed, a table in the dining room, plus cupboard space for your food. This you purchased locally, but sometimes asked the landlady to cook part of it. You were expected to head for the sands straight after breakfast and not ask for more than one bath in the week. Poorer people, especially those with large families, may only have managed a day at the seaside, if that.

Excluding the restrictions of the digs, the week was basically yours to do as you pleased. Scarborough's sands and rock pools were a delight for the bucket-and-spade wielding youngsters. When this activity palled, there were the donkey rides. Sun-worshipping mums and dads basked in deckchairs, or bravely entered the sea, maybe first making use of one of the many bathing machines. Exhilarated, they may have patronised a mussel or oyster stall beside the harbour.

Scarborough was distinguished for its range and quality of entertainments. The Aquarium & People's Palace provided endless indoor treats; the title was a misnomer because, in addition to fish, the bizarre but lavish labyrinth housed a host of diversions. The three-acre underground complex had a café, numerous amusements and shows, including dodgems, a bowling alley, rifle range, band performances and illuminated fountains. It became known as Gala Land and advertised a six-day season ticket. Catlin's Royal Pierrots gave twice-nightly performances at the Arcadia on South Shore. George Royle's Fol-de-Rols performed at the Floral

Hall on the North Side. The Spa became known for fine music. Alick Maclean directed the Spa Orchestra for 24 successive seasons from 1912 onwards. Minstrels and Punch & Judy appeared on the beaches. The Open Air Theatre put on its first production in 1932, *Merrie England,* with a chorus of 250.

An immediate success when introduced in 1931 was the North Bay Miniature Railway, with a scenic coastal route to Scalby Mills. A cruise from the harbour aboard one of the famous steamers such as *Bilsdale*, *Coronia* or *White Lady* was irresistible. The annual cricket festival was incorporated in 1876 and has, over the years, presented some top cricketing names at North Marine Road. Tennis and hockey tournaments, golf weeks and angling festivals became established as yearly highlights.

Scarborough's transport needs were well provided for. The main railway station, which is still in use, was opened in 1845. The big hotels used to provide their own horse bus services to and from the station. To cater for arrival and departure of excursion trains, the North Eastern Railway opened another station in 1908, slightly further inland but now closed.

Day or half-day outings by rail or road were popular. Road transportation was provided by horse-drawn wagonettes and later by motor charabancs. The NER owned a fleet of charabancs which ran from the rail station. A prominent charabanc operator in Scarborough was Robinson's Motors Ltd. They too worked from the station forecourt. Up to fifteen charabancs were sometimes parked there, awaiting the start of tours. Forge Valley or Rievaulx Abbey were favourite destinations.

The Scarborough Tramways Company operated trams from 1904 to 1931. Various parts of the town were covered, including the main railway station. On South Bay, trams ran along the sea front, with a spur traversing the private road to the Spa buildings. The route along North Marine Road was parallel to, but some distance from, the sea front; it terminated near to where Peasholm Park was constructed. The resort and its region had a number of motor bus operators, including Scarborough & District Motor Services and Pioneer. Most of them became prey for the large United Automobile Services, whose buses also replaced the trams. The various cliff tramways (or lifts) were a boon to tired holidaymakers.

The Yorkshire coast was famous for its fish, Whitby and Scarborough being the main coastal ports. At Scarborough, the cobles and trawlers provided a never-ending source of interest as they unloaded their catches, which included cod, haddock, plaice and whiting, plus crabs and lobsters. This was the commercial side of fishing; the leisure aspect included fishing from the piers, the Marine Drive or hiring a boat. Early last century, a small boat for three persons cost around 1s 6d per hour, fishing gear included. The annual herring harvest reached its peak from August onwards. Local trawlers were joined by those from Scotland and other areas, spending several days at sea. Scotch fisher girls moved south with the herring and helped local men to clean and pack the 'silver darlings.'

Unique to Scarborough from 1930 was big game angling for tunny fish. The sport ended in 1954. Although herring fishermen sometimes caught the monsters with improvised harpoons, the British Sea Anglers Federation laid down strict rules for their capture by 'sportsmen.' They had to be caught with rod and line from a rowing boat, without help from the boatman, except when hauling the fish aboard with a gaff.

Most of the illustrations herein are taken from postcards in my own collection, but I am grateful for the loan of a few cards from Simon Smith.

Norman Ellis
June 2007

5. The popularity of Foreshore Road and the adjoining sands is evident here. Sandside, the harbour and Castle Hill are in the distance. The card was posted from the resort to Walsall in July 1905. *"You see I am writing to you at last and am doing it sitting on the beach."*

6. Less hardy mortals could, for 6d, enjoy sea-water bathing in these public swimming baths on Foreshore Road, seen here c.1905. To the left of the Moorish style tower, photographs and postcards are on sale. The Royal Northern Sea Bathing Infirmary is on the right.

7. Discreetly dressed bathers pose for the camera at Scarborough's first outdoor bathing pool, which was opened on South Bay in 1915. The card was posted in August 1921 by a holidaymaker staying at the Granville Hotel, who wrote, *"Having quite a good time but unfortunately weather very bad."*

8. The youngsters seem to be enjoying themselves on the swings. Their clothing and the near-deserted beach suggest a dull day in the 1930s. The thirteen-storey Grand Hotel looms large in the background, an affirmation of Victorian splendour.

9. Entitled *The Fortune of War*, the sand model was constructed on the resort's South Sands, possibly during or shortly after the 1914-18 conflict. The postcard was published by Scarborough photographer AM Cromack.

10. A Wesleyan Methodist Gospel Car is parked by Scarborough's South Foreshore, c.1905, with a Band of Hope meeting in progress. Hymns and object lessons would have been included, with emphasis on pledging to abstain from strong drink. Observe the small harmonium.

11. This lively scene shows the Rotunda Museum, backed by hotels on St Nicholas Cliff, and part of The Grand Hotel on the right. Eyes are on a parade which is delaying the tram as it approaches Falsgrave Road. Alfred M Pepper, photographer, 113 Victoria Road, Scarborough, published the card.

12. The Aquarium & People's Palace was a vast subterranean area at the seaward end of Valley Road. The complex is shown at left (with an entrance) and right on this card, posted in August 1906. Much of the internal style was Indian. The aquatic element was supplemented by an aviary and monkey house.

13. A pair of two-mast fishing vessels rest in East Harbour, with Castle Hill behind. The large four-storey building to right of centre is the old Sea Bathing Infirmary. This and adjacent buildings were demolished to connect Sandside to the new Marine Drive. The card came from Arthur Pilkington's fancy repository on Scarborough's Eastborough.

14. At Sandside, hard-working Scotch fisher girls have attracted an audience of holidaymakers as they clean and sort the herring. West Pier and the fish market are visible in the distance. The card was posted from Scarborough to Rotherham on 30 September 1906.

15. In the early 1900s, Scarborough was Britain's fifth largest herring port. For approximately a ten-week season, Scotch fisher girls followed the fishing fleet down the East Coast. The photographer captured this group on the town's East Pier c.1906.

16. Each girl could gut fifty herrings a minute and sort them into different grades, before they were packed into barrels with ice and salt. Part of the harvest was exported to Russia. This is another postcard from photographer AM Cromack.

17. Fish landed at Scarborough, such as cod, haddock and sole, was auctioned in the fish market on West Pier, as depicted here. Packed with ice, much of it was taken to the railway station for dispatch inland. The card was posted from Scalby to Grosmont in 1906.

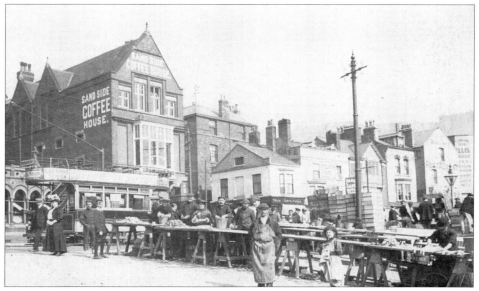

18. Cafes, coffee houses and restaurants are shown along Sandside, pictured here c.1906. Also visible are the trestle stalls selling oysters and other shellfish, and providing salt and vinegar! The tram is nearing its terminus; the return journey was through the town to Scalby Road.

19. An amazing amount of detail is crammed into this panorama of Sandside and West Pier, taken from the lighthouse, c.1937. Visitors found the pier a never-ending source of interest. Perhaps some of them had arrived in the cars parked on the left.

20. Vincent's Pier, shown with its lighthouse, was a departure point for summer steamer excursions. *The Scarborough* (shown), *Nunthorpe* or *Cleveland* used to leave for Whitby via Robin Hood's Bay, or Bridlington and Flamborough Head. Local photographer AM Pepper, Victoria Road, published the card.

Landing Tunny Fish at Scarborough

34   A. Y. Series

21. Interested spectators look on as a tunny fish is landed beside the harbour. The monsters were sometimes placed on show for charity. The British Tunny Club was formed in Scarborough, with headquarters at 1 East Sandgate.

H.R.H. Princess Mary Christening the New Motor Lifeboat "Herbert Joy II" at Scarborough.

22. Scarborough had a succession of lifeboats from 1800 onwards. The first motor lifeboat, called *Herbert Joy*, was presented in 1923 by Alex Joy in memory of his brother, Herbert Joy, who had drowned in the bay. Here, *Herbert Joy II* is being launched by HRH Princess Mary on 5 August 1931.

23. One of Scarborough's best loved steamers, *Coronia*, crosses South Bay with a full complement of passengers. Over the years, the resort's pleasure steamers also included *Royal Lady, White Lady* and *White Lady II*.

24. *Daily Mail* prototype Avro 504 was landed on South Bay at Whitsun 1914 by FP Raynham. The plane was provided with a twin-float undercarriage for landing at coastal resorts. It was later commandeered for war service, but was damaged beyond repair in a crash caused by engine failure in August 1914.

25. A girl called Rene decorated her bicycle as June Roses in one of the Scarborough Carnival weeks. She is on the right of this postcard, produced by the Pictorial Studios at Bland's Cliff and Newborough, Scarborough.

26. For many years, Walker's Studios, Scarborough, visited Scarborough Annual Cricket Festival to photograph the teams. On 1, 2 & 3 September 1937, the MCC team played Yorkshire. The MCC team was (l to r) JM Sims, M Tindall, GO Allen, HM Garland-Wells, RES Wyatt, EH Hendren, CIJ Smith, FR Brown, AD Baxter, DR Wilcox and WHV Levett. Yorkshire won the match by eight wickets, with Herbert Sutcliffe and Len Hutton getting the bulk of the runs in both innings.

27. The South Cliff Gardens were tastefully laid out by Scarborough Corporation, to include the tiered Italian Gardens and the Belvedere Rose Garden, shown here c.1910. The postcard was published by Thomas Taylor & Son, stationers, 37 & 38 Newborough, in their 'Queen' series.

28. Severe storms have periodically devastated the Scarborough sea front. The aftermath of one, c.1905, is pictured. Huge stones from the Spa's retaining wall have been carried some distance. The postcard was retailed by George Wherritt, fancy goods dealer, of 7 Eastborough.

29. Scarborough Spa evolved from the healing mineral springs discovered in 1620. Its buildings, terraces and wooded slopes had no rival on the Yorkshire coast for beauty and enjoyment, and perhaps a bit of snootiness! The main building, left, with its Grand Hall and a theatre, was erected in 1877-80 to replace an earlier structure destroyed by fire.

30. The Spa's bandstand, left, was constructed in 1913 to replace a similar structure. The ballroom on the right dates from 1925. The Spa was purchased by the Corporation in 1957. Both these postcards were published by J Salmon of Sevenoaks, and show watercolour paintings by AR Quinton.

THE FORESHORE ROAD—SCARBOROUGH

31. Thomas Nelson & Sons, book publishers and printers, produced a series of chromo-litho postcard scenes of Victorian Scarborough when its genteel air pervaded. Four of the cards are reproduced. Here, on Foreshore Road, families seem to be enjoying the pleasures of the beach and promenade.

THE NORTH CLIFF—SCARBOROUGH

32. North Bay has an appearance of unspoiled beauty. The pier shown was completed in 1869, to attract more people to this side of the burgeoning resort. It was destroyed by storm in 1905 and never rebuilt.

33. The paddle steamer *Scarborough* is moored alongside Vincent's Pier and the lighthouse. In the left foreground is part of East Pier; in the left background are Cliff (Spa) Bridge and Grand Hotel. The unknown artist has again injected an air of elegance into the picture.

34. From Cliff Bridge, leafy Ramsdale Valley stretches inland and is crossed by Valley Bridge, depicted here. Erected at Scarborough in 1865, this iron bridge had been rescued after it collapsed into the River Ouse at York. A new and wider Valley Bridge was opened in 1928.

35. Ramsdale Valley or Valley Park wanders inland for 600 yards, part natural and part man-made. The upper end of the wooded valley, with its ornamental lake, is depicted on a postcard by AR Quinton, published by J Salmon.

36. Scarborough's fishermen and firemen compete in the annual football match and tug-of-war contest on Boxing Day morning c.1907. The postcard was published by the Yorkshire Gravatone Co of Scarborough.

37. The sorting office at Scarborough GPO on Aberdeen Walk, with postmen about to deliver mail, features on this card, posted from the resort to Birmingham on 16 July 1911. The message relates to one William Taylor who was very ill after an operation for appendicitis.

HOMELESS   SPRING BANK   SCARBORO

38. *"This is a picture of a house blown down with a shell. It is down Seamer Road. The street is called Spring Bank. The children are sat on the remains".* The message relates to shelling from two German battle cruisers and one light cruiser at dawn on 16 December 1914. Nineteen people were killed and eighty wounded.

39. Will Catlin (real name William Fox) came from Leicester, and acquired his first pitch on Scarborough's sands near the Spa in 1894. Catlin's Royal Pierrots are pictured at this location c.1905, on a postcard published by AM Pepper, Scarborough.

40. Catlin's Royal Pierrots (they performed before King Edward VII) are featured at the bottom of Ramshill Road, near the Aquarium. Catlin eventually built Scarborough's famous Arcadia pavilion, and obtained sites in other resorts. In winter, Catlin's Royal Pierrots performed at inland towns such as Leeds and Derby.

41. These Coronation Minstrels performed at the Indian Theatre in the Aquarium. This theatre also presented variety entertainments four or five times a day, with acrobats, bicyclists, conjurors, gymnasts, jugglers and ventriloquists. Boxell & Co, photographers of 44 Victoria Road, Scarborough, published the card.

42. Being two miles from the centre of Scarborough, a motor bus service was eventually provided to take people to the Mere, a sheet of water on the western edge of Oliver's Mount, with boating, fishing and picnicking. Here, hanging baskets adorn the café at the Mere.

43. Facing on to Westborough, part of Scarborough's impressive railway station is featured. Horse carriages ply for hire, whilst, behind the railings, Robinson's advertise their motor charabanc tours. In the background is the Pavilion Hotel, now demolished. Edgar L Scrivens of Doncaster published the card.

44. Three North Eastern Railway charabancs in Scarborough's station forecourt prepare to leave for local beauty spot Forge Valley in 1906. The tiered seats provided good visibility, but the solid tyres gave a bumpy ride, although the speed limit was set at 12 mph. Boxell & Co published the card.

45. From 1904 until 1931, the resort had electric street tramways, operated by Scarborough Tramways Company, but eventually acquired by the Corporation, on whose behalf United Automobile Services substituted motor buses. One of the cars is pictured on opening day, 6 May, beside the railway station. ETW Dennis of Scarborough published this postcard.

46. Tramcar No.14 traverses Falsgrave Road, running in the direction of Scalby Road, and is passing the general store of Haynes & Co on the left. Some of the passengers are probably taking advantage of the 'Round the Town' excursion advertised on the car's dash for 3d.

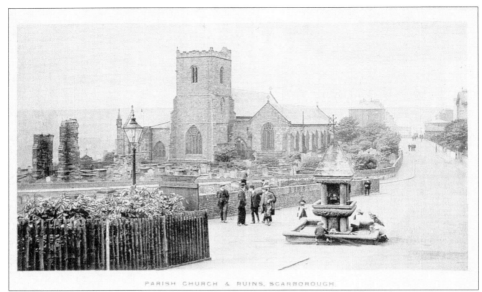

PARISH CHURCH & RUINS, SCARBOROUGH.

47. Located on Castle Road, at the foot of Castle Hill, the Parish Church of St Mary was founded in the 12th century. It was considerably restored in 1850. This postcard was published by Boots Cash Chemists in their 'Pelham Real Photograph' series.

WESTBOROUGH WESLEYAN CHURCH SCARBORO.

48. From small beginnings, nonconformity spread through Scarborough. The Baptists, Congregationalists and various branches of Methodism were represented. Westborough Wesleyan Methodist Church, shown here with its impressive pulpit, organ and gallery, was designed to hold 1,300 persons. The card was posted from the resort to Rothwell Haigh, Leeds, in 1907.

49. The Wesleyan Methodists also built Queen Street Chapel, pictured here c.1907, and of similar internal design to that on Westborough. After being badly damaged by fire in 1915, a new chapel was opened on the same site in March 1923.

50. From humble origins in 1881, the William Boyes Company became a famous drapery business on Queen Street. On 26 February 1915, its remnant warehouse was gutted by fire. The adjacent Queen Street Chapel, shown at rear centre, was severely damaged. The postcard was part of the prolific publisher ETW Dennis's output.

51. The splendid expanse of Scarborough's North Bay is captured on this card, posted from the resort to Alfreton, Derbyshire, with an Edwardian stamp and the simple message, *"Lovely day, hope you are well"*. Much building work eventually occurred on the distant hills around Scalby.

52. Clarence Gardens, shown here c.1905, were created out of the crumbling undercliffe of North Bay in 1887-88. Subsequently, the terraced paths, rustic bridges, bandstand and seating became very popular. Note the parasols.

53. With the tide in, most of the holidaymakers on North Bay, c.1906, are confined to the promenade or small slipway. Hire of bathing huts is available from a ticket office, whilst donkeys wait to provide rides. A remnant of the pier is visible in the distance. Alfred M Pepper, photographer, published the card.

54. Bathing, amateur sand-modelling and cricket appear on this 1930s view of North Bay, but the Punch & Judy show has attracted a group of children. Of Italian origin, the puppet show reached England late in the 17th century and still remains popular.

55. The Promenade Pier on North Bay was opened in 1869, after three years of construction. Elaborate buildings were later added at each end. The pier was destroyed by storm in 1905, as shown on this card, posted from the resort to Dewsbury on 22 July that year.

56. After the pier disaster, the pavilion and shops at the promenade end remained in use for a few years, as pictured. In the background is the newly constructed Marine Drive, officially opened in 1908 after many years of work. This is another postcard by AM Cromack.

57. Corner Café was opened in 1925; this scene was captured in 1934. The crowds along the extended North Bay and family cars along Royal Albert Drive (foreground) suggest a bank holiday. A charabanc and five buses are parked, some of them destined for the railway station. J Bamforth & Co, Holmfirth, published the card.

58. Five cliff tramways (or lifts) were constructed at Scarborough, three on South Bay and two on North. Shortest-lived was below Queen's Parade (1878 to 1887). North Cliff Lift, built near Corner Café, is pictured on a Salmon of Sevenoaks postcard soon after inauguration in1930. It lasted until 1996.

59. Opposite the railway station on Westborough, the Waverley Temperance and Victoria Hotels dominate much of this scene. Nell posted the card to Miss E Arnold of 30 Francis Street, Leeds, on 10 February 1905, stating *"Sorry to be so late in sending you a PPC, but as usual loads of homework. Just off to school now"*.

60. Two decades later, Westborough is pictured looking in the opposite direction. Ethel posted the card to Hogsthorpe, Skegness, on 16 September 1935. *"We arrived safely about quarter to four. Got nice digs on top of cliff. Going for a sea trip to Robin Hood's Bay this afternoon"*.

61. St Nicholas Street is seen from Newborough, with Boots Cash Chemists on the corner. The Nottingham-based firm published the postcard in their 'Pelham Real Photograph' series. Further along, left, is Marshall & Snelgrove's posh department store where, at one time, you had to be suitably dressed to get in.

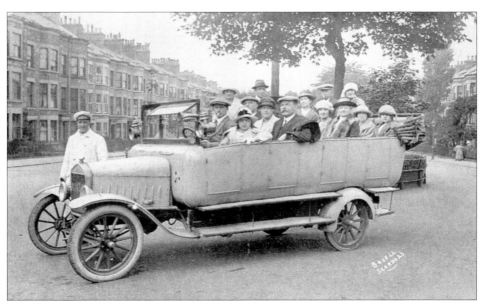

62. The establishments along Trafalgar Square, pictured here, offered board residence or apartments and boasted their nearness to North Bay and Peasholm Park. Photographers Boxell & Co captured the excursionists before their departure, probably hoping to sell a few postcards later.

63. These are some of a long row of guest houses erected on Queen's Parade, overlooking Clarence Gardens on North Bay. They have pleasing front gardens. Some of the establishments have signs for apartments; others provided full board.

64. More holiday accommodation is shown on tree-lined Columbus Ravine, running down to Peasholm Park. The Baptist Church on the left was erected in 1915. The school uniforms, and especially the caps, are typical of the 1930s.

68. Scarborough's scenic North Bay Miniature Railway was opened in 1931, running from Peasholm Station at Northstead Manor Gardens to Scalby Mills. Here, diesel-powered Neptune (Pacific No 1931) is captured on camera in its early days on a J Salmon postcard.

67. Peasholm Park was created in 1911-12. This scene was captured on official opening day. The Mayoress, who had cut the ribbon to proclaim the park open, is just left of centre with her bouquet. The park's development continued between the wars, including the Peasholm Glen extension.

65. The Crown Stores of Bamforth & Co, provision merchants, are pictured at the corner of Seamer Road and West Bank, with Falsgrave Park in the background. A Mr Holts took the photograph in 1906, and attracted an audience of children, some of whose parents patronised the shop.

66. With mature trees and a wide pavement, Falsgrave Road is shown in the 1930s, looking east from near (New) Park Road. Falsgrave Post Office is on the right, selling cigarettes, sweets and postcards. Charles N Jamson of Doncaster included the card in his 'Empire View' range.